Thank you so much for purchasing this book

I would like to dedicate this book to all of my bosses who have supported me throughout my life and influenced me to keep pushing forward.

Laura, Lynette, and Cynthia

BEHIND THE MAKING OF THE BABY TRUMP TOUR

BY: Didier Jimenez Castro Editors: Laura Swanson – Carole Thompson Cover Artist: Mike Patten

My name is Didier Jimenez-Castro. I am an activist and social advocate. As the middle child of five growing up in Hillsborough, NJ, I was taught by my mother early on about the importance of compassion and finding happiness by helping others.

Volunteering began early for us. When I was young, my family and many of our neighbors would meet to clean garbage from the local streams and roads. I would also visit with a sickly, older man in my neighborhood. When I turned 16, I started getting involved with many non-profit organizations. My father drove me to the Make-A-Wish Headquarters in Monroe Township, N.J. in April of 2013, and as soon I as walked in, I knew I wanted to volunteer. The tour guide for the headquarters made it clear from the moment I entered that they were utterly committed to bringing happiness to kids with life-threatening conditions.

My part-time job throughout high school was at a local supermarket. While working there, I was able to raise awareness and funds for foundations such as Autism Speaks and Partners in Caring. I was also featured on a Cheerios box along with my fellow supermarket employees because, together, we helped raise over $1 million to fight hunger in our community through the company's charity initiative. When I was 27, I organized a fundraiser called The World's Biggest Water Balloon Fight in Hillsborough, with all proceeds going to Make-A-Wish.

In February of 2016, I heard of a man named Bernie Sanders from Vermont who was running for President. I agreed with his views about election reform and putting an end to mass incarceration. I felt an incredible amount of passion for his message, so when I heard that he was speaking at Rutgers University, only a twenty-minute drive from my home; I knew I had to be there.

It was the first political event I had ever attended, and his platform was exponentially more powerful than any of the other candidates'. This 74-year-old man instantly became an inspiration to me, and at 28, I knew I had to emulate him and use my voice to educate the American people on important issues that affect all of us.

Subsequently, I volunteered at his campaign headquarters in New Jersey, where I made friends with many of my fellow progressives. I also volunteered with the local Congressional campaign for Peter Jacob for Congress, who ran against Leonard Lance in New Jersey's 7th District in 2016.

Meanwhile, I continued to work full-time at my job at a homeless shelter. By working with the less fortunate, I saw firsthand what happens when the government makes cuts to programs like Medicaid, food stamps, and child health initiatives. With my eyes opened, I was that much more motivated to act and speak out against the injustice that is happening in this nation.

    I decided to be creative and wanted to start a movement that people could get excited about, one that would really grab everyone's attention. With the constant, distressing news cycle, we needed something that would get folks out of their comfort zones without adding more negativity to their lives, which brings me to how my friend Jim Garvin and I started the Baby Trump Tour.

    On Thursday, July 12, 2018, I was watching the news when I saw a picture of the Baby Trump Balloon that was scheduled to fly in London for the President's visit the next day. I immediately knew we needed that balloon here in the United States; I wondered if I would have the time and resources to get the balloon across the Atlantic. I needed a partner in order to take this on.

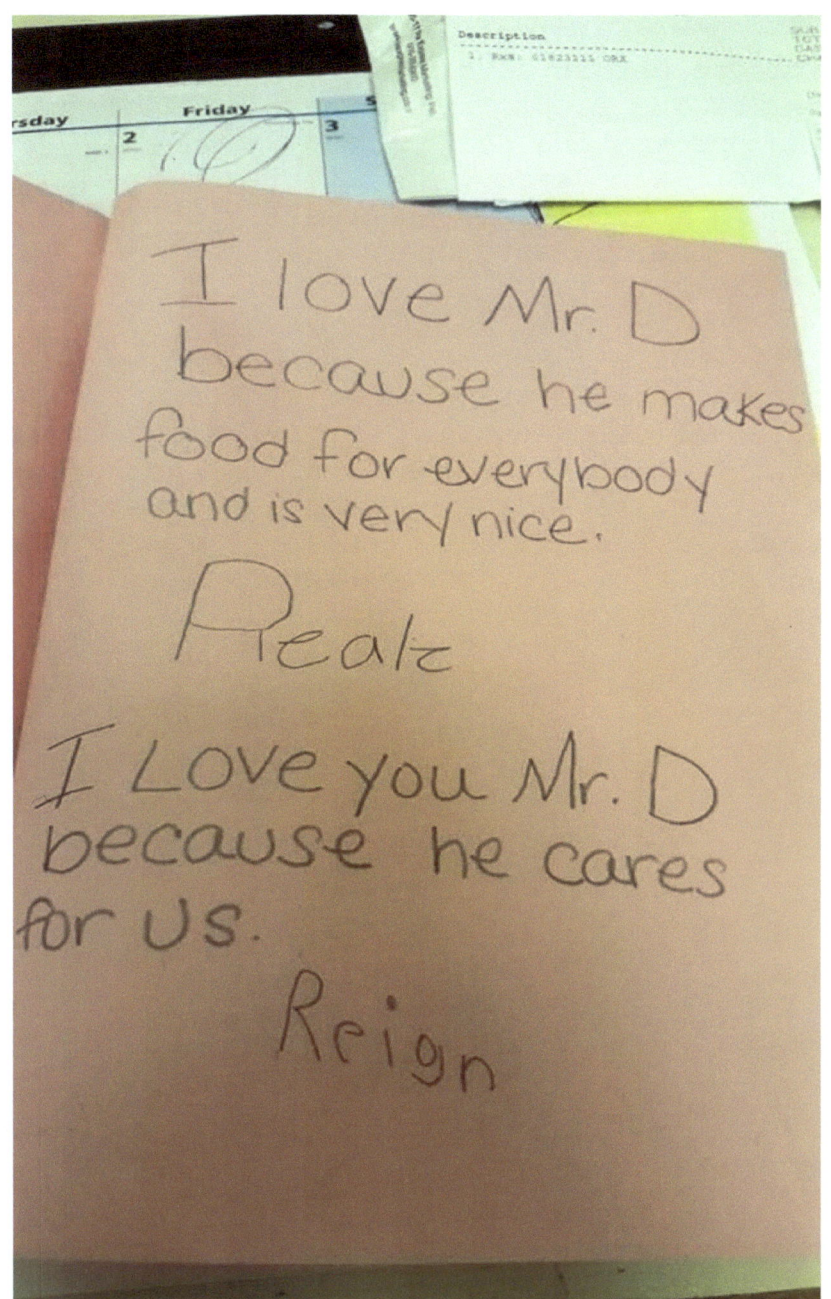

(Note given to Didier by child in shelter)

Through social media activist groups, I was able to get in touch with Jim Garvin, founder of The People's Motorcade. The group had been protesting near Donald Trump's Bedminster, New Jersey, golf course since he'd been sworn into office. As an activist, I respected the protest and the message they were relaying.

The People's Motorcade is focused on calling out the President's lies, including his destructive executive laws on immigration, and financial policies that exploit the lower and middle classes. The protestors drive a motorcade with signs back and forth across the entrance to the golf course every weekend to declare their opposition to this administration.

(Didier Jimenez Castro and Jim Garvin awaiting Baby Trump delivery)

In order to gauge the demand for a Baby Trump in the U.S., I created a poll in the activist group NJ 11th for Change on Facebook. 24 hours later, the feedback was overwhelming. Americans wanted Baby Trump to come to the United States. The very next day, Jim and I spoke on the phone for about 30 minutes and immediately hit it off, committing to work together. On Saturday I joined Jim at the weekly People's Motorcade protest, where we made it official; Baby Trump was coming to the USA.

On the evening of Saturday, July 13th, I started a GoFundMe page with a goal of $4,000. By Sunday morning, we had raised over $7,000. The media started contacting me directly through Facebook and email. I was flabbergasted by the number of messages and phone calls I received.

I never thought it would reach so many people so quickly. Word spread nationwide and the response was amazing. Later that morning, I called Jim and told him I thought we had something really special on our hands. Journalists from major, national publications began calling me for interviews, and the GoFundMe had reached over $10,000 by Sunday evening.

Little did we know, our lives were quickly going to change. I felt like a celebrity. Wherever I went people recognized me. "Hey, how's the balloon doing?" they'd say, or, "I saw you in the newspaper. When is the balloon going to be here?" People had become invested in the campaign, both emotionally and financially. Overnight, this had become much bigger and more impactful than I could have ever hoped for.

By Monday morning we had donations from all over the country, some even made in the name of Ivanka Trump! With the massive amount of support and attention we were receiving, I knew that it was only a matter of time before we would be harassed by Trump supporters. I was right. Somehow, they found out where I was working and began calling my superiors, painting a picture of lies about my representation of the organization. As a result, my supervisor pulled me aside and warned me not to have my name connected with any anti-trump campaigns, or where I worked. I quickly realized I needed someone else to be a spokesman for this project if I was going to keep my job, so I notified Jim and he became the official spokesman for the campaign.

While all of this was going on, our GoFundMe continued receiving donations. By Wednesday, July 18th, we had raised over $24,000, and decided at that point to stop accepting money. In the days that followed, we received a number of threatening emails, and somebody sent us an article about a Somerset resident, Kathie Kitt, who was raising money to pay for potential bail after she planned to pop the balloon.

GoFundMe does not allow its users to raise money for any illegal activity, especially bail for destroying private property. Following the deletion of her GoFundMe account, Kathie refused to speak to the media. "I don't want to talk to the press," she said, "they always twist things."

After doing my research, contacting the UK Baby Trump campaign, and reading various articles about the event, I was able to find the name of the manufacturer who had worked with the activists in London. The activists, however, wanted to take a few weeks to recharge their batteries before jumping back into assisting a new campaign, so we decided to act locally instead, knowing that time was of the essence.

Jim and I found a manufacturer in California who was eager to jump on board. Within a week, our manufacturer had begun work on a total of six Baby Trump Blimps that Jim had ordered. The London Baby Trump activists saw how quickly we were moving forward and jumped on board at that point, providing a huge amount of support. They understood time was on not on our side, so they connected us with key activists and progressive organizations located in the States. We are forever grateful for their role in making the Baby Trump Tour so successful.

Throughout this time, we received close to a thousand emails from people worldwide asking for a Baby Trump Blimp to come to their hometowns and cities. We quickly realized we would need to recruit more talent in order to help us manage such a large number of requests, both for volunteering and press. Our reach on social media grew each day, and we tried our best to get back to everyone. We knew we needed to keep our relationships open and honest with the press and our followers in order to keep the momentum going.

Although we were passionate about spreading the word, Jim and I both agreed to exclude Fox News altogether, because we knew that their interviewers would pander to their ratings and viewers, doing everything they could to drag us through the mud. Avoiding them, we decided, was the best course of action.

At this time, Jim was doing all of the interviews. He had the time and the passion and I couldn't have had a better partner in this crazy scheme. I call it crazy because the World Wide Web does not have a tutorial on how to start a blimp tour in national protest, and we had to think outside of the box in order to create one. I wouldn't have been able to go through the ups and downs that come with starting a project of this magnitude were it not for the support of my girlfriend, Erin, who really helped me push through.

My sister reached out a lot during this time, spooked by the high level of exposure my name was getting and fearing the backlash would damage my life. Ever the realist, she understood that Trump supporters carry a lot of hate and urged me to take precautions. There was a lot of anxiety on both our parts, because it was impossible to predict how far Trump supporters were willing to go to stop us. However, I believe that I had the greater motivator.

Every day on my 30-minute drive home from the shelter, I would get my motivation thinking about the children who were staying there. I could see how badly these kids desired a road to higher education not rattled by debt. I was painfully aware of how their lack of affordable healthcare affected their quality of life. I knew how much all of these kids and their families would benefit from taking back Congress from the Republican majority, and I wanted to do my part in making it happen.

On Thursday, August 9th, Jim gave me a call letting me know that our first two Baby Trumps were arriving in Bedminster. I borrowed a friend's pickup truck and met Jim to pick up 'the twins.' My girlfriend recorded our journey from breakfast – where we hashed out the details of our first event
– to us picking up the boxes together and taking them to Jim's house. Eagerly, we opened one of the boxes and found the manual. We regarded that collection of papers like new parents would a birth certificate.

Once everything looked perfect and Jim was able to safely store our blimps, we left with big smiles on our faces, thinking of the next steps.

Jim put a team together to do a test inflate, most of whom consisted of retired baby boomers. As the youngest member of the team, I was incredibly happy to finally meet everyone, and it was inspiring to see baby boomers and millennials working together. It was this camaraderie that spurred our search for volunteers, especially those with professional experience who could up the quality of the project.

Towards the end of August, I started feeling drained from work, politics, and in my personal life, but I didn't want to lose my motivation to succeed at something so meaningful. My girlfriend, noticing this, helped me set up a nice dinner at a local restaurant for friends and family just before my birthday. I was surprised by a couple of activist friends as well as a local Hillsborough candidate. She gave me a Trump piñata and candy to fill it, which had to be the most interesting gift I had ever received. I brought it to the shelter (after removing the face), drew a new face on it, and let the kids go wild. My mother finally got to meet Jim, which was a great feeling of unity for me, and it had a profoundly energizing effect on my drive.

    A couple of days later, Jim called and told me he'd found the perfect place for our test flight, coincidentally landing on my birthday! We kept the address and homeowner's information private and only allowed ten people onto the property.

    The drive to the house was 40 minutes away, and although I'm no morning person, I hopped out of bed that day with spirits soaring. It was a beautiful, cloudless day in Califon, N.J., as we gathered at 10 AM in a private, acres-large backyard for the first flight.

The balloon team laid out a tarp with sandbags on every corner and sides followed by the Baby Trump in the middle. We all shook hands, chatted for a bit, and then got right back to work. We started the inflation with a leaf blower and then switched to helium. We had a professional with us to help us properly inflate the blimp. After two and a half tanks of helium, we used the leaf blower again for one final fill. The first Baby Trump Blimp was ready and boy did he look good up there.

The entire experience was so unique and rewarding. Everyone had worked so hard to get to this point, and more importantly, we all got along. Looking up at Baby Trump, it was hard not to smile (regardless of political affiliation). There's nothing like a little humor to bring people closer together. A photographer from the Washington Post was there, and he did his best to get candid shots of me as I walked around answering questions from the press. One of the teammates brought champagne, and we toasted our test flight and each other.

While it felt a bit strange to be getting so much attention, I was and am proud of the work that I've done, and hope that I can serve as a powerful role model to others. In just over a month, we managed to raise close to $25,000, order six Baby Trump Blimps, and create The Baby Trump Tour organization. One of our primary responsibilities would be to train activists around the country to hold these events properly and safely.

    I believe one of the reasons the project worked so well was the way we built our social media handles around it. My strong resume in fundraising and volunteer-work gave the campaign legs and kept the donations pouring in long after reaching our intended goal.

    Building a strong relationship with journalists and producers helped the project reach the national spotlight, and that's the beauty of having the free press. Finding a right-hand man like Jim Garvin to help me out with the chaotic process of answering hundreds of emails, calls, and interviews was a blessing. Jim, now retired, has a lot more time to get hands-on, especially when it came to recruiting new members for specific jobs that required professional experience. We are very lucky he found folks with real motivation to change the world and willing to donate their time to help lift this project off the ground.

On September 4th, Jim and I got to pick up the remaining four Baby Trumps, which brought the final number to six Baby Trumps in our control and ready to tour the country. The relationship with the original creators of the Baby Trump improved vastly in the weeks leading up to our final pick up, and I am indebted to them for their genius idea. France may have given us the Statue of Liberty, but England gave us Baby Trump, and for that I am forever grateful.

(Photo by Olivia Holmes)

When things get tough in our personal lives is when our allies truly shine, those who come to our rescue when we need the support the most. The people of England have demonstrated with their protests that they stand with us against our morally corrupt President and administration. What a crazy time to be alive, with the President of the United States of America tweeting around the clock and Mueller moving closer by the day. Sometimes I worry I might get pulled over by a cop who is a Trump supporter who recognizes my name and acts biased towards me, seeing as I happen to live in a very Republican county. I am no longer surprised at casual co-workers who feel strongly opposed to what I do, and they make sure to tell me about it.

At the end of the day, regardless of how they feel, the truth is that I am just a 30-year-old wanting to better the world for all of us with a giant balloon and a very popular progressive agenda. I can't honestly go to work at the shelter and later go home and forget about the injustice that is happening in my backyard.

The goal is not just the removal of Trump but an overhaul of the entire, broken system that has been in place since long before he took office. Getting the most progressive candidates possible elected nationwide this November is a good way to move us in that direction. People won't leave the comfort of their air-conditioned homes to an open field to meet any, unknown, progressive candidate.

This is the really important work we hope to achieve with Baby Trump rallies across the nation. It's the lure of seeing the now-infamous Baby Trump that gets people out onto the streets, but the true win is the education on both local and national politics that we're able to achieve as a result.

Progressive candidates are often running against Republicans who take millions from special interest groups and 'dark money' from Super-PACs. This injection of money gives them the ability to spend thousands on radio, TV, and newspaper ads, and more recently, online advertising. A progressive candidate is at a major disadvantage because a progressive only takes money from their constituents, each with a $2,700 limit.

Their pledge not to take special interest money makes it possible for them to ignore the requests of powerful, greedy corporations once in Congress. One way to deal with that financial disparity is to create events that bring regular Americans out to meet their local progressive candidates. Baby Trump rallies give them a huge stage to lay out their policies and interact with the local community. Alexandra Ortasio Cortez has proven that strong grassroots efforts can defeat candidates who align themselves with powerful corporations and Super-PACs.

I want to make it clear that anyone who is determined enough can create a movement that helps combat those administrations whose main goal is to dismantle the safety net of the poor and working classes.

I got behind spearheading this project because I believe humor is a great tool to push a message across without bringing people down or hurting feelings. In this day and age, there are so many tools at our disposal to affect real, lasting change. All we have to do is care enough to use them.

In the end, no matter what, you will still get heat from Trump supporters. You just have to follow your heart in the end and be smart with every curveball they throw at you.

Every other week I like to visit right-wing news outlets on social media and go through the hateful comments about the tour. Sometimes I get upset reading what these folks are saying but at the end of the day, you have to find the courage to go forward in spite of it. The positive messages overshadow the ignorant comments, but it will still blow your mind seeing how far these folks can go. It can bog you down if you aren't conscious of its effect on you.

This project chips away at your mental state, so in my situation I realized having the support of my girlfriend and her pug Bo makes things a little less crazy. I work two jobs, at times doing two shifts in a row with little to no time to relax.

I work continuously on the project on my phone during any free time I do get, and when I finally get home, I am greeted by a loving pug and a wonderful woman. I wouldn't be able to do any of this without their support, like Erin helping me problem-solve any number of issues and helping Jim record tutorial videos for the project.

At this point, we are upgrading the website and making it easier to navigate. I love the features we integrated into it, and it has a ton of potential when it comes to message and reach. It blew my mind how Jim and his friends were able to create materials, tutorials, and posters from scratch. Those materials made it possible for us to start this tour at such a high level. Let me remind you, everyone is volunteering to make this possible. These folks are putting hundreds of hours into building the foundation of the tour(s). At the end of the day, as silly as this sounds, teamwork does make the dream work and we are a great example of that. If only the White House were as dynamic as we have been, maybe then the situation we're in wouldn't be so dire.

We are about a week from shipping the balloons to a couple of cities and our teams around the country are getting everything set for them.

These kits will contain the balloon and everything they possibly need to bring that balloon up and going.

While we don't ship the helium tanks or the leaf blower, we give them full instructions and requirements from members of the group to fulfill. Once their event is over, it gets shipped to a different location. We predict a large attendance at every event, a prediction backed by the thousands of messages we've gotten through both email and social media. I have to constantly carry a cell phone charger because these days, my phone does not stop buzzing. It doesn't bother me though, because it means things are moving forward.

There are so many decisions to be made and tons of work ahead of us. It really looks like there is no end to this huge mess in D.C. I fear it will take centuries of work to fix, but we have to start somewhere. The only thing worse than doing something and failing, is doing nothing at all, wondering what you could have achieved if you had tried.

As it stands now, Florida has a Baby Trump to bring awareness to the storm that destroyed Puerto Rico a year ago. The Baby Trump will continue to stay in Florida in order to help people like Andrew Guillen, who is a progressive Democrat running against the Republican candidate Ron DeSantis. We hope to replicate events like this all over the country and bring awareness to much-needed progressive candidates and noble causes.

Now I would like to discuss why we ended up with Donald J. Trump as the President of the United States. I don't want to sound like a broken record, but I believe the Democratic Party as a whole failed the middle class and the poor. Now, most of you will say, "oh boy here we go with that finger-pointing, Didier. Wouldn't you rather unite us for the November elections?" Well, I have a response. I am on the same team, but it's important to deal with our issues head-on and not ignore our faults.

    For years, the Democratic Party has been in the pocket of Wall Street, bluntly doing their bidding in Congress. Both Republicans and Democrats have worked together over the years to help the rich get away with corporate welfare abuse and a lopsided tax code that lets the ultra-rich keep their amassed wealth virtually tax free. The only way to make a drastic change right away is to overrule the Citizens United v. FEC ruling, which basically says that money equals voice and that the ultra-rich can form Super PACs with potentially dirty money. The Supreme Court has ruled that in some cases, corporations are people and they can donate an enormous amount of money to both candidates and Super PACS. Corrupt CEOs and greedy corporations need to be put in check and held accountable to the American people, but that will never happen while they maintain control of our elections with their bank accounts.

Furthermore, the media needs to be held accountable for the $2 billion worth of free press it gave Donald Trump, disproportionately spreading his hateful message nationally and internationally in pursuit of ratings and revenue. Meanwhile, candidates like Bernie Sanders had trouble getting any attention for their campaigns, in spite of massive popularity and sold-out rallies.
The media basically gave the bad guy his own live stream into the homes and lives of millions of Americans. I was so put off by the media during that time that I spearheaded a protest at the NBC headquarters in August of 2016. I felt the need to call out their blatant bias towards certain candidates. Protesting their unethical journalism felt like a gift, and it just so happened to be on my birthday. I was accompanied by a number of activists from all over New York City, as well as some New Jersey folks from back home.

In 2016, when we found out about the corruption within the leadership of the DNC, it became clear that Bernie Sanders' loss was a result of that collusion.

When you work against Bernie Sanders, you are not hurting just him and his campaign, but you are hurting his fast-growing base and the chance for Americans to unify against a true threat to our democracy.

We cannot be Stronger Together if you sucker punch your teammate and respond to it with amnesia. We could have had this election in the bag, but I think at the end of the day we had to learn a lesson about the importance of having a true democratic process. We cannot have superdelegates in the Democratic Party. We can't stand behind any party that lets the wealthy and ultra-rich dictate the policies for the middle class and the poor.

The reason I wrote this book and decided to give you a glimpse into the birth of the Baby Trump tour is oddly specific. I want folks like yourself to find that courage from deep inside, and to follow through. Standing up to corruption nationally and locally is necessary for a healthy democracy to exist. I went through a lot in this project, but I am honestly telling you that it is always worth it. Seeing immigrant children in cages at empty Walmart is the straw that broke the camel's back. It was in that moment that I knew I had to act quickly on a challenging plan and to find others who were like-minded.

Thinking outside of the box and taking risks are necessary in the world we live in, but getting up again after we fall only hardens our resolve.

I truly understand why so many of us are feeling down and like we don't have the power to change the way things are going. The constant barrage of news about the blatant, shameless corruption within the Trump administration and those who are suffering as a result can make even the most idealistic American lose hope. However, the only time to act is now and we need to organize and come together, first with our neighbors and then continue on from there, because real change comes from the bottom up. Democracy is an ideal that we should never surrender and it's up to us to fix it. These are some serious times and I have to hold on to the hope we can overcome all of these hurdles in our current government. Everything is temporary, even the bad times, so we just have to fight hard and hang on tight.

Thank you so much for buying this book and for letting me share my story with you. I hope it becomes a call to arms for you and yours to get out there and fight for the kind of world you want to live in.

The Revolution Continues.

SPECIAL THANKS TO EVERYONE WHO HELPED ME PUT
THIS BOOK TOGETHER

www.ingramcontent.com/pod-product-compliance
Lightning Source LLC
LaVergne TN
LVHW010021070426
835507LV00001B/28